_To_

MW01101452

# SPARK WORDS

## A **POWERFUL** APPROACH
## TO AFFIRMATION SUCCESS

_May Magic Angel
You have so much
to LOOK forward to—_

_Love & Blessings_

_Anne Marie_

_Sept 7, 2022_

# Dr. Anne Marie Evers

_May all yours dreams come True!_

Affirmations International Publishing Company,
North Vancouver, British Columbia

Printed 2018 in USA
Affirmations International Publishing Company

ISBN 978-1-926995-11-3

Queries Regarding Rights and Permissions
Affirmations International Publishing Company,
4559 Underwood Avenue,
North Vancouver, Canada V7K 2S3

Email:      annemarieevers@shaw.ca
Fax:        604-904-1127


Websites:  www.annemarieevers.com
           www.annemariesangelchapel.com
           www.heretohelpsolutions.com
           www.selfimprovementtalkradio.com
           www.kidspower.ca
           Pictures courtesy of Cards of Life
           www.cardsoflife.com


Design & book production:
           Michael Gordon Brouillet
           Designtree Studio
           www.designtreestudio.ca

# Message from the Author

**WELCOME** to the Wonderful, Magical World
of **Spark Words and Spark Word Combos,**
Where Dreams Really Can and <u>**Do**</u> **Come True!**

When You Change your Thoughts and Words —
You Change Your Life!

Message from Your
Affirmation Doctor Anne Marie Evers

I am so excited to share with you some very powerful and unique information. The book that you are reading is a very special book that contains priceless information and one that can become your constant companion because the information, teachings and processes are within you! I have just recently been using this special Spark Word information, and the results are amazing.

I feel like I have been given a very special and precious gift that keeps on giving. I have actually been teaching the power of properly done Affirmations, Affirmation Life Tools and Short Form Affirmations for many years and I just realized that I have been teaching these very Spark Words for years. The only difference is that I call them Short Form Affirmations.

## IMPORTANT TO ADD THE SAFETY CLAUSE –

## 'TO THE GOOD OF ALL PARTIES CONCERNED'

When I told a friend about this *Spark Word Process* and the wonderful miracles manifesting for others and myself, he listened very intently and then he said, "Wow! What you are telling me is so exciting and wonderful that it is almost *'scary!'*

I totally agreed with him and I told him that is why we add the above safety clause, *'to the good of all parties concerned'* and this includes everyone and everything and of course YOU!

This safety clause forms a part of your Intention (Master Affirmation).

# Spark Words

## A POWERFUL APPROACH
## TO AFFIRMATION SUCCESS

After years of teaching readers, friends and clients, I began searching for a quicker way to make affirmations work. I read about James Manham's switch words and I decided to make my very own 'Spark Words' by putting into action some of the Short Form Affirmations that I have been teaching for many years. They worked and are working beautifully. I am so happy to share them with you. These Spark Word Combos are actually a *continuation* of the Affirmation Program that creates a powerful pathway to a quicker, sometimes instant manifestation.

Now I feel it is time to make my Spark Word Process stand on its own, using principles and information from my 35+ years of teaching Master Affirmations, Short Form Affirmations, Affirmation Life Tools and much more.

This process will never wear out or go out of style. This wonderful power lies within you! You can access it any time you wish, and wherever you go. And it doesn't require a suitcase!

## SOME OF MY CHALLENGES

Trouble sleeping
Craving sweets constantly
Releasing excess weight
Challenge with finding files and wasting time

These simple, powerful words (Spark Word Combos) set off a spark within me as I started using them with fantastic sometimes magical results. It is my hope, prayer, wish and affirmation that as you read this book, it will create a similar **spark** within you.

## SMORGASBORD OF LIFE

When reading and studying this information, please keep an open mind.

## A PARACHUTE IS NO GOOD UNLESS IT OPENS!

Allow yourself to think in new ways. Be open and responsive to new ideas, ventures and exciting, new Spark Word Paths—the beginning of fulfillment of your fondest and deepest dreams. Repeat often—"I am a Powerful Spark Word Magnet!"

Journeying through life is like visiting a delicious smorgasbord. When you go to a buffet dinner or smorgasbord, you are not waited on. *You have to get up and get whatever you want – yourself!* You decide what you want to eat and then take the appropriate action of putting that particular food on your tray or table. This is similar to making decisions in your life, choosing what Life Tools, (Spark Word Combos) that you wish to use to create, and to bring about positive changes in your life such as —

Good health
Positive, uplifting friends
Abundant wealth
A perfect, lasting, successful career
Forgiveness
Special love partner
Self-esteem
Family harmony in your life and much more

Don't be like some people who just sit back and wait saying: "God/Creator will give it to me when He decides." I believe God gave us brains and minds to think, to empower us to make wise decisions as well as the gift of 'free will and discernment.' Perhaps it is time to start taking responsibility for our thoughts, words and actions.

Could it be time for you to dust off 'Your Magic Wand?'

Please share your success stories with me. I am always delighted to hear from my readers and others. Should you have any questions about this unique process, please email me at annemarieevers@shaw.ca

# DISCLAIMER

This Spark Word Book's purpose is to give you information on different thoughts, ideas, methods, Affirmations, Affirmation Life Tools, Short Form Affirmations, Spark Words and/or Spark Word Combos and how to use them to help you in all phases of your life journey.

This information is based on my life experiences over the years and from testimonials, letters, emails, phone calls and personal visits from many of my readers and others worldwide who have used these wonderful Life Tools with great success.

Of course, the results differ with each individual depending on how much time, energy and excitement is put into creating and repeating these Spark Word Combos and also on the person's individual belief system.

If you are on medication, please check with your health practitioner and in any case use the information, Affirmations and/or Spark Word Life Tools, etc. as *additives* . . . always adding your own down-to-earth, common sense.

**MY SPARK WORD COMBO
FOR YOU IS**

## TOGETHER  MIRACLE

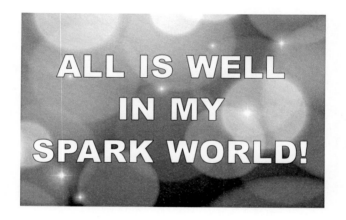

## HAPPY SPARKING!

With Love and Affirmation / Spark Word Blessings,

Dr. Anne Marie Evers / **Dr. Spark!**

# Prayer for a Friend

I said a prayer for you today and know God must have heard

I felt the answer in my heart, although He spoke no word

I did not ask for wealth or fame, I knew you would not mind

I asked Him to send treasures of a far more lasting kind

I asked that He be near you at the start of each new day

To grant you blessings and friends to share your way

I asked for happiness for you in all things great and small

But it was for His loving care for you, my friend

I prayed most of all!

*Author Unknown*

# Dedication and Appreciation

I wish to dedicate this book to my wonderful Affirmation Family at Silver Harbour Senior Centre where I lecture monthly and have been for the past ten years. And to my dear friend Anita MacAulay, all my readers, Radio/Internet listeners, clients, associates, friends and family who have been faithfully doing affirmations with me for many years.

As well to all the people who attend my regular monthly lectures at Evergreen House, North Vancouver, BC *(part of Lions Gate Hospital)* on <u>70 Ways to Cope with Negative Side Effects of Chemo and/or other Medical Treatments</u>.

## *I WISH TO THANK THE FOLLOWING WONDERFUL FRIENDS AND COLLEAGUES*

**Ruth Ellen Peters** for all her help, ideas and encouragement throughout this book to bring it to its completion. We brainstormed and came up with the words *'Spark Words'* and it created a spark within us and the Spark Word Combo was born!

**Christine Einarson** for her continuous, much appreciated help with this book and many of my affirmation projects.

**Rebecca Haynes** for her fresh and new ideas, her enthusiasm and support. I am so happy to reconnect with her. We are both cancer/chemo survivors and found that powerful Health Affirmations supported us! Now these powerful Spark Word Combos help us on our healing journeys.

**Wynnae Huizinga Seldon,** Evergreen House Social Worker, North Vancouver, BC for the many hours she spent editing this book.

**Roxanne Davies,** a friend and colleague for her great suggestions and editing work. Roxanne was a newspaper reporter in Montreal and Vancouver. Today, she writes corporate profiles for employee newsletters as well as essays for the Globe and Mail newspaper. She met thousands of people in the course of her career and believes every life can be a work of art. She authored a 350-page family memoir entitled Orchards, Crossroads and Dreams and co-authored Olga, The OK Way with 95 year-old master athlete, Olga Kotelko.

She is currently writing a book for a retired Canadian TV cameraman. Roxanne is passionate about helping people leave a written legacy for their families. You can contact Roxanne Davies at arttales@telus.net

**Carole Matthews,** well known Intuitive and Talk Show Host, who believes in me and practices the power of affirmations. She always supports me in my projects. She is a guest on my Radio Talk Show and I am a guest on hers. http://carolematthewsintuitive.com

Carole and I were on air speaking about Spark Words and the Spark Word Combos, using an example of words to go to sleep quickly — **TOGETHER MIRACLE – OFF**. When I came to the word **OFF**, Carole started yawning on air! She was quite embarrassed and began to apologize and struggled against the feeling to yawn.

We agreed just how powerful words are and the physical effect that they can have upon us. Carole is now using this Spark Word Combo to help her sleep soundly and restfully at night, together with other Spark Word Combos with continued success.

**Cameron Steele** and his lovely wife Lucia, owners and producers of www.ctrnetwork.com for their faith in me and my Affirmation Program, Affirmation Life Tools and more. Their support over the past 10+ years of broadcasting my weekly Dr. Anne Marie Evers Show has been invaluable; now they find my *Spark Word Combos* very interesting. Thank you, thank you, thank you, Lucia and Cameron.

**Caroline Ryker**, my life-long friend who continually uses Affirmations, Affirmation Life Tools and now Spark Word Combos with great success. I am so proud of her accomplishments and positive mental attitude, that she so willingly shares with everyone.

**J. D. Michaels** for all the assistance offered.

## THE MAGIC OF THOUGHT

Magic is the intelligent use of thought forces. The process of repeating your Spark Words and/or Spark Word Combos over and over is like the sprinkling of magical powder of enhancement, energy and power into the air to bring your desires to you.

You create with every thought you think and every word you speak.

## YOU ARE A POWERFUL THOUGHT MAGNET!

I am so happy to share this wonderful, powerful and yes, 'Magical Spark Word Process' with everyone!

## HAPPY SPARKING!

# Foreword

## CAROLINE RYKER ON SPARK WORDS!

It is with great pleasure that I write this foreword. I have known Anne Marie Evers for 38 years. Anne and I worked together in Real Estate in Canada for years and together we affirmed listings and sales and we both became very successful members of the Canada Permanent Leader Club.

Her first book, <u>Affirmations Your Passport to Happiness</u>, I have used faithfully. Over the years, I have kept a three-ring binder of the affirmations that I have written with great success . . . such as: affirming for love, marriage, buying a house, selling a house, traveling, and material things. I also used them for my cancer operation/chemo recovery and much more.

## MANIFESTED AFFIRMATIONS

I watched as Anne Marie created and blew breath into many of her affirmations over the years that have manifested and I witnessed her many successes. She also has a three-ring binder of her successes and she is the author of many books and e-books on the power of properly done affirmations.

She is also a colon cancer/chemo survivor. Her husband Reg passed away of a massive heart attack during her chemo treatments. One of the Oncologists at Lions Gate Hospital asked her if she would be interested in sharing her methods and ways of keeping going and being so positive even in negative, stressful situations. He asked her if she would like to share positive, uplifting information with other patients going through similar health challenges. For the past 3 years she has been lecturing monthly at the hospital to chemo patients, their families, friends and caregivers with wonderful success.

Her latest book, <u>70 Ways to Cope with Chemo and/or Other Medical Treatments</u> is available on amazon.com with her other books and e-books.

## COMPLETED SPARK WORD COMBO BOOK

This Spark Words and Spark Word Combo Book provides a short way of doing affirmations. You still need to do your Intention (Affirmation), but Spark Words and Spark Word Combos can be recited quickly with great success.

I believe this simple, yet effective and proven Spark Word and/or Spark Word Combo Process is becoming one of the cutting-edge tools in Health Care as well as making positive changes in every part of your life.

Anne Marie is a wonderful person who gives of her time spreading hope freely and helping people.

This book on Spark Words will make all your dreams come true, if it is good for you and others.

Anne Marie always stresses that we add what she calls the safety clause 'to the good of all parties concerned' to **ALL** of your Intentions, Affirmations and Spark Word Combos.

This is a very important part of the Process and ensures that what you are affirming is good for you as well as others.

Start today and see how quickly this 'Magical Process' works for you!

Happy Sparking!

Caroline Ryker, Arizona, USA

# TABLE OF CONTENTS

# Chapter One

# 5 W's and 5 Building Blocks of the Spark Word Combo Process

## WELCOME TO THE WONDERFUL WORLD OF SPARK WORDS, SPARK WORD COMBOS AND THE SPARK WORD PROCESS, WHERE DREAMS REALLY CAN AND DO COME TRUE!

**W**ouldn't it be great to have a Magic Wand to make your wishes come true? Now you have *just* that – a Magic Wand called *Spark Words*! These words create the spark that turns on the switch within your subconscious mind that turns on the light and energy to create what you wish to obtain, be or do.

Words that mean certain things to you and your desires become symbols in your subconscious mind.

***NOW YOU HAVE THAT MAGIC WAND AND MORE!***

It is important to become aware of the marvelous, incredible power within. If you do not become aware of this power and the wonderful gifts you have and are working with, how can you be grateful for them? Gratitude that is filled with feeling is very powerful and has a very high vibration that is present in **every** Spark Word and/or Spark Word Combo. It is very important to say, "Thank you, thank you, thank you," after repeating each Spark Word Combo Request.

## PART 1

# THE 5 W's OF SPARK WORDS AND/OR SPARK WORD COMBOS

## WHAT

Spark Words are Short Form Affirmations, commands or decrees that are easy to remember and are repeated over and over for quick manifestation.

These powerful Spark Words create symbols of your desire in your subconscious mind and **BYPASS** your conscious, objective, reasoning mind going directly and immediately into your subconscious mind without argument, disagreement or rationalization from the conscious mind. They attract your wishes (desires) to you and help you gain inspiration and wisdom from within.

They also clear the path of all obstructions and/or negativity so that your Spark Word Combo Request can manifest easily for you – and sometimes instantly!

## SPARK WORD COMBOS

Spark Word Combos consist of phrases that join several Spark Words together, that become very powerful as each Spark Word has its own individual energy and creative power. When you join two or more Spark Words, your Spark Word Combo becomes even more powerful because of the added energy and power.

When using Spark Words for a specific desire or a purpose, you simply need to affirm or chant them and they work exactly as their name suggests . . . like a spark that ignites the powerful energy switch within, that manifests your desire. I call this process 'A Powerful or Laser Approach' to my very successful Affirmation Program.

## WHERE

You can read over and repeat your Spark Words and/or Spark Word Combos anywhere at all, while exercising, walking, waiting in line, waiting for a friend at a café or while stuck in a traffic jam and . . . just anywhere!

## WHEN

You can also repeat your Spark Word Combos any time at all. Please remember to glance over your Intention (Master Affirmation) and *then* repeat your Spark Word Combo Request.

## WHO

Any person can design their own Spark Word Combos and repeat them over and over. I have an eight-year- old girl and a great, great grandmother doing the Spark Word Combo Process. Now the great, great grandmother is doing them mostly for the health and happiness of her family and self.

## WHY

Why do this Process in the first place?

Create and repeat the Spark Word Process to realize your fondest dreams, wishes and affirmations. We do them to attract the people, abundant health, careers, relationships, family harmony, self-esteem, peace of mind, money, material things, spiritual growth and much more.

This Spark Word Combo Process, which is a *continuation* of the Affirmation Program that I teach is built on 5 powerful Building Blocks. These 5 Building Blocks provide a solid and firm foundation upon which this Spark Word Combo Process is built.

## PART 2

*1st Building Block*

# FORGIVENESS

## REAL TRUE FORGIVENESS HEALS EVEN THE DEEPEST OF WOUNDS

To forgive mostly and truly benefits the person doing the forgiving. Forgiveness is a choice—and so is *not* forgiving. When you do not forgive another person, you remain energetically connected or tied to them. When you forgive others, you break those ties and allow them to move on with their lives—and for you to move on with yours. Forgiveness is love in action.

True forgiveness reduces stress, lowers blood pressure,

increases well-being and promotes good health. Forgiveness is the first and most important Building Block or step to start your Spark Word Combo Process. It releases negativity and provides a clear pathway for your Spark Word Combo Process to manifest your desires quickly and easily.

Stop beating yourself up for your *'so-called'* true failures. I believe that there is no such thing as failure. Failure according to what? Failure according to whom? I use my 'so-called' failures as *extra-ordinary* fertilizer for my many successes.

## 2nd Building Block

# POWER of THOUGHTS

## YOUR THOUGHTS BECOME THINGS

I believe that the greatest power that has ever been discovered is not nuclear energy, nor the power of wealth or fame. I believe it is the power of your thoughts and mind. Thought is creative and it is the first and most crucial stage in the development of any new idea, invention, business or other venture that becomes reality.

Thoughts become living things. When thoughts are held in the mind, they form a life of their own and attract other similar thoughts. Your powerful, positive thoughts create certain symbols of Spark Words in your subconscious mind that work especially well to attract your deepest desires.

## 3rd *Building Block*

# MIND POWER

## CONSCIOUS AND SUBCONSCIOUS MIND

The processes of the human mind constitute one of the greatest unsolved mysteries of the great Universe, yet most of us take our minds very much for granted. We think, act and live, rarely stopping to reflect on how the mind works or how we control it.

Affirmations, Spark Words, whereby we repeatedly state our desires become imprinted upon the subconscious mind and represent *'The Master Key to Unlocking the Door'* to Mind Power.

We have one mind with two distinct yet interrelated functional characteristics.

One is the conscious, objective, outward or waking state. The other is the subconscious, subjective, inward or sleeping state.

I liken the conscious mind to the captain of a ship who gives the orders and the subconscious mind to the crew who immediately and without question obey the captain's orders. How are you instructing your subconscious mind? When creating and repeating your Spark Words, you are contacting and working with your magnificent subconscious mind. Your subconscious mind takes you at your word. Your mind is unique and your Spark Word Process will be unique.

## 4th Building Block

# AFFIRMATIONS, SPARK WORDS
## YOUR ORDER TO THE UNIVERSE

Spark Words, like Affirmations, are similar to prayers, wishes or goals, only they are more structured and specific.

To affirm is to make firm and simply put, the basis of all Affirmations, Spark Words and Spark Word Combos is positive thinking.

Your positive, well-thought out and specific Affirmation becomes your Intention, which is the first step to creating the appropriate Spark Word Symbols in your subconscious mind that manifest your desires.

When placing your order with the Universe, be very specific, saying exactly what you desire. Then gratefully take delivery of your desire.

## *5th Building Block*

# CREATIVE VISUALIZATION

## STEPPING AHEAD INTO THE FUTURE

When creating and repeating your Spark Word Combo, it is not absolutely necessary to use creative visualization. However, I use it in my own Spark Word Combo Process and I find it works quicker for me.

The images your mind receives from your mental world are just as real as an event actually taking place. When you practise creative visualization, you are transporting yourself into the future. You are putting yourself into a situation that has not yet taken place. Since your mind does not know the difference between a real event and an imagined event, it accepts your visualization as truth.

## HAVE FUN CREATING YOUR
## OWN SPARK WORDS

Experiment with what words will become your individual Spark Words and/or Spark Word Combos. It is also wonderful to have sample copies to get ideas from. Please remember the ones that you create from your inner self become the Spark Words that work miracles for you in creating powerful symbols in your subconscious mind that bring about the manifestation of your desires.

Every person is different. You may wish to substitute words that you feel more in tune with . . . ones that resonate with you on various levels. I personally find at times that 2 Spark Words work the same for a particular desire.

## *For example:*

When I did the Spark Word Combo –

## TOGETHER – MIRACLE

The Spark Words **ON** and **PROJECT DONE** worked with exactly the same results!

They created the same image in my subconscious mind that manifested in my reality.

You are the only Decision Maker and Creator in your world and this is your life! Create it as *you* wish.

# THE SPARK WORD COMBO PROCESS WORKS WITHIN THE LAW OF ATTRACTION

More gathers more

Like attracts like

What you think about you bring about

What you are seeking is seeking you!

*Spark Words When Properly Done, Always Work!*
*(Sometimes instantly)*

# Chapter Two

# Brain Memory Mind and More

**M**emory is our ability to encode, store, retain and then to recall information and past experiences in the brain.

We use memories from past experiences to affect or influence what we are doing today and we can thereby learn from unsuccessful methods, ways, etc. and change direction.

Spark Words and/or Spark Word Combos are the symbols that you have created in your subconscious mind which are stored there, waiting to be used by you. When the Spark Word Process that you choose is repeated over and over, you access those particular symbols that work for you – sometimes instantly!

You are increasing and encouraging your brainpower to become more active. When you use The Spark Word Process over and over, you create the framework for your subconscious mind to remember and reaccess that symbol and your Intention, Affirmation, wish or prayer manifests, sometimes like 'pure magic!'

# IMPORTANT NOTE

In memory there are no words, as it is visual and auditory. Spark Words do not require visualization. This is an important factor for people who have difficulty with creative visualizing.

Unlike the Affirmation Process, Spark Word Combos work successfully *without* using creative visualization. It is your choice whether or not to incorporate it into your Spark Word Combo Process. Personally, I prefer to use creative visualization.

## THE MORE YOU PRACTICE
## THE MORE SPARK WORDS WORK!

With Spark Words, like any other method or practice, the more you practice and work with them, the more efficient they become.

Be patient and let go of any rigid attachment to the *outcome* and soon you will discover that you are becoming a 'Spark Word Expert' creating on higher levels and manifesting things that you never, ever imagined possible. Remember that each Spark Word creates a symbol that has energy and power all of its own. Just think of all the times you can use your brilliant, creative process to attract and keep your fondest wishes and desires, whether they are physical, spiritual or material!

# SUBCONSCIOUS MIND

Think of your mind as a high-speed computerized library of contents. Within your subconscious mind you have infinite wisdom and a limitless power supply just waiting to be accessed and used by you. It is never short of ideas! You cannot see your mind, but you know you have a mind. You cannot see life, but you know you are alive. You cannot see electricity, but you must believe in it because you pay your hydro bills regularly.

Your subconscious mind never sleeps. It is always on the job. Really think about it. How are you instructing your subconscious mind?

Your subconscious mind's actual function is to give thought its physical shape in the material world and manifest as affirmed. It is important to learn how to use this unlimited, inexhaustible power to create your heart's desires.

## WHAT IS CONSCIOUSNESS?

To do this requires consciousness – a state of mindful awareness, alertness and aliveness in the present moment. You become what you are in life from what you are in consciousness. To be conscious is to think and to think is to give form to thought. With a positive focus, you attract good things and happy experiences to you.

When you lower your consciousness, you give away your power and attract situations, thoughts, events and people that reinforce this lack of power.

## IMPACT ON YOUR SUBCONSCIOUS MIND

*I read somewhere . . .*

### APPROXIMATE

**J**ust Reading............................................................ 10-15%

**R**eading and picturing............................................ 55-65%

**W**riting, reading, picturing, feeling
and practicing creative visualization
and concentrated imagery ................................... 100%

## YOU ARE THE CREATOR AND ONLY DECISION MAKER IN YOUR UNIVERSE!

When you think, you actually issue a command or order and your subconscious mind, your humble servant, always ready to obey your command, goes to work immediately to make it happen as affirmed. Nothing is impossible. You control the thoughts you think and transmit into your subconscious mind, which, in turn, is part of the Universal Mind.

The world *within* creates the world *without*. Everything you find in your world *without* was first created in your world *within*.

Even that chair you are sitting on, or the computer you are using was once a thought in the mind of someone. Now they are in a physical form that you can have, use and enjoy.

You cannot jump into another person's mind and think their thoughts for them, nor can anyone jump into your mind and think your thoughts for you.

You, and you alone are in total control of what you think, say and do.

**HAPPY SPARKING!**

*Spark Words When Properly Done, Always Work!*
*(Sometimes instantly)*

# Chapter Three

# About the Spark Word Combo Process

## CREATING WITH THE SPARK WORD COMBO PROCESS

You create and shape your life with your thoughts. All things that become part of your physical reality are first created in the mind from the raw material called thought. Because it is an instrument of thought, the Spark Word Process is a powerful tool that you can use to help shape your life as you choose. Spark Words are powerful words used to connect directly to your subconscious mind and give it direction for bringing your desire to you.

## YOUR INNER GUIDANCE SYSTEM

It is important to listen to your Inner Guidance System and the more you listen and follow the suggestions and directions from it, the more magical and efficient your Spark Words become to you.

Spark Words inform your mind of a desire or experience

that you wish to have by creating that particular symbol in your subconscious mind that represents your desire.

And remember this process completely **bypasses** the objective, reasoning conscious mind. It just manifests!

It is so exciting that immediately upon repeating your Spark Word Combos with powerful intention, your Internal Guidance System together with your subconscious mind, begin to find ways and outlets to create and attract that desire or situation to you. Then it is your job, and yours alone, to become aware of any ideas, hints, suggestions, thoughts or promptings that you receive from them and act on the ones that resonate with you.

One of the functions of your subconscious mind is to take the thought, which is wonderful, pure energy and give it physical shape in the material world. When you think a thought, you issue a command or decree. Your subconscious mind manifests the thought in the physical world where it becomes the things and events in your life.

Change your thought patterns and you change your life. Every time you work with this process you are creating an inner belief that it works and it does. You JUST KNOW! It is important to decide just what Spark Words or Spark Word Combos that you will use for a particular desire and the more you repeat and use it, the quicker the manifestation.

It works because you become more aware of what that particular Spark Word Symbol means to your subconscious mind.

## THE BRIDGE

Spark Words create a bridge between your desire, your subconscious mind and the manifestation that you desire. Spark Words have their own timeframe and as I mentioned earlier, you may discover that a particular Spark Word or Spark Word Combo works quicker than others.

Spark Word Requests or orders can take time or they can manifest instantly. This depends on the time, energy and focus that you put into studying this process and how much you actually practise using this Spark Word Combo Process.

Many people have amazing results even when they do not believe in the Spark Word Process.

## CHILDREN HAVE SPARK WORDS
## ALL OF THEIR OWN

Children learn very early about the power of Spark Words. They say words like, "No! Oh no! Please, milk, up, down, sit, eat, stop, look, don't, doggie, kitty, bad, good," and many more.

*Spark Words When Properly Done, Always Work!*
*(Sometimes instantly)*

## *Chapter Four*

# Intention Your Master Affirmation

## HOW TO CREATE YOUR SPARK WORD COMBOS

**Y**our Intention, (Master Affirmation) is your desire that you wish to 'spark' for. Your Spark Words are also called Short Form Affirmations. In your Intention, please make sure your desire is very specific and affirms exactly what you want. Remember - *This is Your Order to the Universe!*

## STEP PROCESS

## STEP 1

# RELAX AND DECIDE

Relax in a comfortable place, go within, take several deep breaths and decide exactly what you desire to have, be or do. In order to create, have and use the Spark Word Process successfully, you need to first write out your Intention. Your *Master Affirmation* is your Intention, which you only create and write once, *(similar to your Last Will and Testament)*. Make this as specific as you can. Really think about what it is that you desire.

Record your Intention (Master Affirmation) on your desktop; tablet; or smart phone. You can record it as your screensaver on any one of these devices. You can even record, your Master Affirmation in your own voice, and replay it on one of these devices throughout the day.

You may choose to email yourself your Intention throughout the day to keep it on the front burner of your mind. Each Intention has its own **separate** Index Card or is recorded on the device of your choice.

## STEP 2

# CREATE YOUR INTENTION

## SAMPLE INTENTION (Master Affirmation)

## CAREER

I, (your name), deserve and now have the perfect, lasting, successful, harmonious career that gives me in excess of $ _____ per month or year (net or gross). I am happy and fulfilled to the good of all parties concerned. Thank you, thank you, thank you.

I fully accept

Signed _____ Dated _____

## *Note*

*Fill in the amount of money you desire and then sign and date your Intention.*

When creating your Intention (Master Affirmation), be sure to add the 3 P's – **P**ersonal, **P**ositive and **P**resent Tense.

Create a separate Intention as above for each Spark Word Combo Request.

When you fill in the amount of money, date and sign this Intention, you have made a firm and binding contract with God/Creator, Universal Mind, Higher Self, Universal Power or whomever you believe in.

Add the safety clause 'to the good of all parties concerned.'

Say, "Thank you, thank you, thank you." It is very powerful and important to give thanks in advance. I believe it obligates the planet for more and/or opens the Flood Gates of Heaven for even more blessings. Now that you have created your Intention, it is time to design and work with your Spark Word Combo Process.

While using your device or holding your Picture Spark Word Combo Request in your hand, simply glance at it. You don't have to spend a great deal of time reading or studying it as your subconscious mind takes in every detail at a glance and stores it for all time.

Start repeating your Spark Word Combo. I count on each finger up and down which gives me 20 times and then I add 1 to make 21 times to conclude the counting process.

When you believe that your Spark Words will work and trust that what you are wishing (affirming) for will be delivered to you, it gives energy to your manifestation. Even a small amount of belief works wonders!

## TIME PROCESS

It should only take you 5 to 10 minutes in the morning and the same in the evening to get wondrous results. Remember that you need to blow breath into your Spark Word Combo Process and this is done by taking the above action.

This wonderful process can and does at times work instantly and other times it may take a little longer. Again the more frequently you do it, the more the process works for you!

# TAKING ACTION

You can stand in an elevator all day and affirm that it moves to the 3rd floor. Nothing happens until you or someone else pushes the button to the 3rd floor. This is called *blowing breath into your Affirmations and Spark Word Combos.*

## THE IMPORTANCE OF REPETITION

Repetition accelerates the energy and vibration already present to make your Spark Word Requests manifest more quickly. We have heard it said that repetition is the *mother of learning*. When you repeat your Spark Word Combos, thought patterns are impressed on your subconscious mind. You are transforming your previously held beliefs, opinions, ideas and concepts about that request.

When you say your Spark Word Combo over and over, the words become a living presence in your awareness and your subconscious mind. Later, you become the words in the Spark Word Requests. It is important to then turn it over to a Higher Power—God for materialization. Repetition reinforces the belief system and convinces the mind that it is true. The Laws of the great Universe take care of the rest.

Repetition is accepted in every culture. Some forms of prayer are repeated many times. When people chant in rhythm, it helps them achieve a reflective state. The process of creating and repeating your Spark Word Combos is not a one-time procedure or event. It requires constant repetition.

Make your Spark Word Combos concrete. Think, write, feel and say them out loud with great feeling. Convince yourself of its truth and reality. There is no quick-fix or Spiritual fast-food method of doing your Intention (Master Affirmation) and Spark Word Combo. It takes work, effort and concentration. The results are well worth the effort.

## HELPFUL HINTS

Always affirm in the now. In the mind principle, there is no time or space. Everything is happening in the present moment . . . (now). Never be concerned about the modus operandi. You know the WHAT and God/ Creator, Universal Mind, Higher Power or whomever you believe in, knows the HOW! Stop wasting time worrying about the *modus operandi* (trying to figure out how it will manifest for you). Just *KNOW IT **IS** MANIFESTING!*

## SPARK WORD COMBO REQUEST BOOK

I suggest that you keep a record *(Completed Spark Word Combo Requests)* of the miracles that take place in your life in a special book. When you start a new Spark Word

Combo, it is always wise to review the many miracles that have taken place as they provide you with a certain amount of belief and confidence that the present one will work as well.

I recommend that you start with no more than 3 separate Spark Word Combo Requests and remember to do each one separately and completely before moving on to the next one. I do about 8 at one session, but I worked up to that amount slowly. Always glance at your Intention for that particular Spark Word Combo Request *before* you start the Process.

Really think about what you desire, and make certain it is not something another person wants for you. This is **YOUR** Spark Word Combo Process!

## NOTE

It is very important to include the safety clause, 'to the good of all parties concerned,' to **All** of your Intentions. This is a very important part of the whole process.

*Spark Words* operate through vibration. Say, sing or chant these words. They change your body's vibration so that they resonate at the same frequency of your Spark Word Combo Request.

*Spark Words When Properly Done, Always Work!*
*(Sometimes instantly)*

# *Chapter Five*

# Using the 2 Frame Words – Together And Miracle with Spark Words

**W**hen 'sparking' for health I use the following –

There are two 'Constant Master Frame Words' that *always* stay the same and are used in *every Spark Word Combo*.

These words are –

## TOGETHER and MIRACLE

Master Frame Spark Words enhance and give power and energy to the Spark Word Combo Process.

*In the sample below* **BE HEALTHY** *would be your Spark Words!* And again, Spark Words are Short Form Affirmations, commands or decrees that are quick to learn, easy to remember and ones that are repeated over and over for quick manifestation.

# BRING IN YOUR 5 PHYSICAL SENSES

**See** - Look at the Device or Spark Word Picture Index Card when repeating your Spark Words

**Hear** - yourself repeating your Spark Word Combo

**Feel** - the Spark Word Picture Index Card in your hand

**Smell** - I would also suggest putting a drop of cologne or essential oil on your Spark Word Picture Index Card for the sense of Smell. To complete the fifth sense . . .

**Taste** - a drink of fresh, sparkling water

By adding your 5 physical senses to your Spark Word Combo, you give it extra energy and power for great and quick manifestation.

## SAMPLE SPARK WORD COMBO REVIEW

### 1st CONSTANT MASTER SPARK WORD – TOGETHER

It can also be called *'The Master Key.'* Everyone and everything is working together, including your conscious and subconscious mind and every part of your body to make your Spark Word Combos manifest to your highest good.

### 2nd CONSTANT MASTER SPARK WORD – MIRACLE

This is the miracle of your desire manifesting as affirmed ('sparked').

## THE 3rd IS YOUR DESIRE – THE ACTUAL SPARK WORDS – 'BE HEALTHY'

**TO RECAP**

String the 2 CONSTANT FRAME SPARK WORDS **TOGETHER** and **MIRACLE** with your Spark Words

**IT BECOMES 'TOGETHER MIRACLE – BE HEALTHY.'**

By stringing these powerful words together, you have made the most powerful and unique combination using the power and energy of *each* word.

Use Your Spark Word Combo Tools often and experience for yourself the wondrous manifestation of your fondest dreams!

### TOGETHER MIRACLE – BE HEALTHY

*Spark Words When Properly Done, Always Work!*
*(Sometimes instantly)*

*The Magic of Spark Words*

# MY PERSONAL SPARK WORD COMBO EXAMPLES

## SHORT FORM INTENTION SUGGESTION
## BE HEALTHY

I, Anne Marie Evers, deserve and now attract and maintain radiant health!

**Sample Spark Word Combo**

## TOGETHER MIRACLE – BE HEALTHY!

These 2 words **BE HEALTHY** are your Spark Words.

Remember to repeat the Spark Word Repetition Process 21 times – first thing in the morning and again just before bedtime. It takes 21 days to make a habit.

## ADDITIONAL WAYS SPARK WORDS AND/OR SPARK WORD COMBOS HELP . . .

Heal, attain and maintain abundant health
Create positive character changes
Attract that perfect, lasting, successful career
Attract and enjoy money/prosperity of all kinds
Attract that special, loving, lasting relationship
and/or happy marriage

Forgive and promote family harmony
Improve self-esteem and self-confidence
Find lost things and remember names and events
Reduce excess fat and weight from the right places
on your body
Cut down on starchy foods
Cut Sweets

Cope with and handle medical treatments
Find appropriate help for the grieving process
Attract and maintain Peace and Spiritual Growth in
all aspects of life

To further enforce your *Spark Word Process*, repeat it
over and over until you feel your energy shift

The purpose of Spark Words is to create conditions for success and there is still energy work to do on your part.

You are simply *'priming the pump'* of your subconscious mind for success.

Think of the Spark Word Process as a **short cut** and **powerful approach** to access specific information that is stored in your subconscious mind, just waiting to be accessed and used by you when required for ALL aspects of your life. Study the Spark Words and/or Spark Word Combos and choose the ones you wish to work with for your particular desire.

## OPTION

Later in this book I provide some sample Spark Word Index Picture Cards so you can photocopy the images, print them off and glue them onto Index Cards.

## TO RECAP

Look at the Picture Index Card twice daily, while repeating your Spark Word Combo 21 times.

Now let's review your Intentions (Master Affirmations).

*Remember the old saying that a picture is worth a thousand words!*

# HEALTHY SLEEP

## SAMPLE INTENTION (Master Affirmation)

## OFF – HEALTHY SLEEP

I, Anne Marie Evers, deserve and now have perfect, healthy, sound and restful sleep. I am becoming more and more relaxed and peaceful while drifting off to sleep. I wake up feeling refreshed and rested.

I wake up excited to greet the brand, new day. I am happy to the good of all parties concerned. Thank you, thank you, thank you.

Signed_____ Dated _____

**MY EXPERIENCE**

After using this Intention for two months--No more tossing and turning, no sleep medicines, no counting sheep. Now it is just me and my Spark Word, OFF! I make it my Intention to wake up feeling refreshed and excited about greeting the brand, new day!

Sample Spark Word Combo

## TOGETHER MIRACLE–**OFF or SLEEP**!

This one word **'OFF' is your Spark Word**
You could substitute or add the Spark Word **SLEEP**

# CUT/REDUCE SWEETS

## SAMPLE INTENTION (Master Affirmation)

### CUT SWEETS

I, Anne Marie Evers, deserve and now cut out my cravings for excess sweets. All cravings leave my body now and I am in control of my desires. Rich desserts, chocolates, candy, butterscotch sundaes and fudge no longer tempt me.

I am so excited and thankful. I eat nourishing food that keeps me healthy. I am balanced, peaceful and happy to the good of all parties concerned. Thank you, thank you, thank you. I fully accept.

Signed_____ Dated _____

## MY EXPERIENCE

I have always used sweets as my reward. When I became a business woman, I used sweets after a successful meeting to reward myself. When I realized that excess sweets were not healthy for me, I started using this Spark Word Combo and I discovered, much to my surprise that **All** my desire for sweets left me! All cravings for sweets completely disappeared, something I never thought possible! And for me -- this **IS** a *Divine Miracle!*

### Sample Spark Word Combo

### TOGETHER MIRACLE**–CUT SWEETS**!

# PROJECT WORK COMPLETION

## SAMPLE INTENTION (Master Affirmation)

## ON

I, Anne Marie Evers, deserve and now get things done easily and effortlessly in the specified timeframes. I am in control of my life. I complete all my projects on time.

I have and enjoy the feeling of total accomplishment and I am Right-On! I follow my rule Order of Importance. I am procrastination-free to the good of all parties concerned. Thank you, thank you, thank you.

Signed_____ Dated _____

## MY EXPERIENCE

I use this one almost daily and I find that I accomplish so much more than I did previously. I can feel the wonderful, exciting energy filling every part of my body. Using this process, I am totally amazed at how much I can and do accomplish daily.

Should you be feeling overwhelmed, please do try this TODAY!

Sample Spark Word Combo

## TOGETHER MIRACLE—ON!

# ATTRACT AND KEEP MONEY
## SAMPLE INTENTION (Master Affirmation)
### COUNTING IN

I use the word counting as one of my Spark Words because that is what I do when I receive a large sum of money (cash). I count it.

I, Anne Marie Evers, deserve and now have money in my hand to count that is mine! I am becoming prosperous and I have and enjoy a healthy bank account. All my bills are paid with substantial money left over. I attract money/prosperity to the good of all parties concerned. Thank you, thank you, thank you. I fully accept.

Signed_____ Dated _____

**MY EXPERIENCE**

I repeated the Spark Word Combo, **Together Miracle – COUNTING** over and over and it worked perfectly – **the wrong way**! Money was going out. My washer quit, hot water heater needed repairs, computer crashed, my car required new tires and more. I was confused and then the thought struck me – 'Why not add the two letter word IN and see what happens?' I added that small word **IN** and money stopped going OUT and started coming **IN** from unexpected sources.

Sample Spark Word Combo
## TOGETHER MIRACLE – **COUNTING IN!**

**MY SPARK WORD COMBO**
**FOR YOU IS**

## TOGETHER   MIRACLE

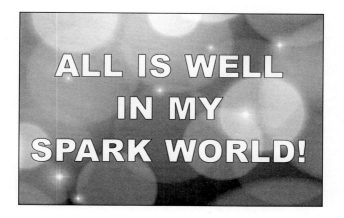

## HAPPY SPARKING!

With Love and Affirmation / Spark Word Blessings

# Chapter Six

# Anne Marie's Personal Spark Word Library

**H**ere is a list of possible Spark Words. Make up your own list using words that resonate with you. Think of what you want and use the Spark Words to receive your desires.

Remember to read your written Intention *before* you start the Spark Word Repetition Process. Also have fun making up your very own, powerful Spark Words.

## NOTE

Because you are only communicating with your subconscious mind, it is not really necessary that you add, 'me and I.' Some readers like to add them for greater certainty.

Pick the Spark Words and/or Spark Word Combos that resonate with you and the ones that you feel comfortable with. You may need to substitute, delete or add your own Spark Words to the list below. This is *your 'Sparking Process'* so make it special, exciting and real.

# WORDS

We create with every word we speak. How are we conversing with ourselves and others? Are we setting up negative conditions or positive ones?

I believe any words can become your Spark Word Symbols in your subconscious mind and that one Spark Word or Spark Word Combo may work quicker than others for certain people. The most important factors are that they resonate with you at the deepest level and they need to be in a similar vibration energy to your subconscious mind. These words should also be in harmony with your Inner Guidance System, body, mind and spirit.

See for yourself how it works. We all have special words that we resonate with. Some words can make us feel sad and others can uplift and encourage us. I suggest that you enjoy experimenting and discover your own truth and the process that works for you.

## SPARK WORD LIBRARY

# TIME TO VISIT

## ANNE MARIE'S PERSONAL SPARK WORD LIBRARY

Spend as much time in the library as you wish, jotting down your own Spark Words. These are suggested Spark Words that you can weave together to make your very own *Spark Word Combos* and/or substitute your Spark Words. The door to the Library is always **OPEN**!

Some of the following suggestions are part of Short Form Affirmations taken from my book, <u>Affirmations Your Passport to Happiness</u>, 8th edition and my other Affirmation Books - available on www.amazon.com

Never underestimate the power of a *'softly whispered Spark Word Combo'* filled with love, excitement and expectancy!

Now may be the time for you to take your Life off 'Lay-Away' and create and attract things, conditions, people and your heart's desires.

Look over the following words that could become your very own Spark Words and/or Spark Word Combos.

Please use the following list as a *platform for launching* your new and powerful Spark Word Process.

Locate the subject below that you wish to work with and

pick the sample Spark Words that work for you. After you have glanced over your Intention, (Master Affirmation) have fun with creating your own Spark Word Combos.

## SOME SUGGESTED SPARK WORDS
## WRITE YOUR 'OWN' SPARK WORDS
## 1% Solution

You can make this percentage any number that is believable to you when *'Sparking'*

## ANNE MARIE'S PERSONAL SPARK
## WORD LIBRARY

1% healthier than yesterday
1% less pain than yesterday
1% happier than yesterday
1% wealthier than yesterday

(Note - When you get to 100%, affirm 'continued radiant health, continued abundant wealth,' etc.)

## CREATING YOU OWN SPARK WORD COMBOS

Choose one of the following statements and make that your Spark Words.

## ADDICTIONS
Alcohol, Drugs, Tobacco, Gambling, etc.
- negative additions going, going, gone!
- control of my body actions
- addiction free
- healthy body, mind and spirit

## AFFIRMATIONS
- specific and believable
- my order to the Universe
- safety clause -- the good of all
- personal, positive, present tense
- saying exactly what I want, not what someone else wants for me

## ANGER *When you put a 'd' in front of anger you get danger*
- free of anger
- balanced, happy and peaceful
- control of my thoughts, words and actions
- healthy body, mind and spirit
- free of negative energy

## BALANCE
- balanced and secure
- control of my thoughts, words and actions
- healthy body, mind and spirit
- grounded and stable

# CAREER

- successful, lasting, harmonious career
- in excess of $ _____ monthly or yearly
- perfect location
- appreciative employers
- using my creative abilities and gifts

# CHILDREN

- healthy, happy and balanced children
- positive money flow for education
- family harmony and respect
- many healthy and balanced friends
- appreciate education

# DEPRESSION

- depression-free
- focusing on positive and happy events
- living in the now
- becoming balanced, healthy and stable
- emotional/medical help accepted

# FAMILY LOVE

- family love and harmony
- spreading love and happiness everywhere
- forgiving self, others and situations
- cancel, cancel negative situations – filling empty space with love
- living gratefully in the now

# FORGIVENESS

- forgiving everyone and everything that hurt me
- forgiving self, others and situations
- loving, respect and approve of self
- living gratefully in the now
- letting go of past hurts and disappointments

# LOVE

- lovable, loving and loved
- loving respect and approve of self
- forgiving myself and others
- happy, harmonious marriage/relationship
- happy, harmonious family

# MIND

- strong, healthy mind
- exciting new ideas and suggestions
- creative ideas
- attracting my desires

# MONEY

- attracting financial abundance
- counting **IN**
- extra money for my desires
- happy and exciting vacations
- powerful money magnet
- my bills paid with money left over

# NEGATIVITY

- cancel, cancel negativity

- safe and protected
- cut negativity
- living in now
- positive, uplifting attitude

## PAIN
- all pain leaves my body
- pain-free and happy
- enjoying and loving my healthy body
- relaxed and happy me now
- becoming healthier and healthier

## RELATIONSHIP
- lasting, loving relationship/marriage
- compatible, healthy life partner
- kind, loving and respectful
- financially independent
- sharing mutual interests
- living happily together

## SLEEP – Close Eyes
- repeating, '**OFF**' over and over
- healthy, sound and restful sleep
- waking up happy to greet the new day
- tossing and turning in bed – Gone!
- sleeping medication – Gone!
- counting sheep – Gone!
- Just my **OFF** and I
- waking up rested and excited

## SELF-ESTEEM
- forgive myself
- taking care of myself
- enjoying self-approval and love
- loving, respecting and approving of self
- accepting myself just as I am

## THOUGHTS
- happy, positive thoughts
- new creative thoughts
- exciting and new ideas
- finding balanced solutions
- believing in myself and my future

## WORRY – (Useless emotion)
- worry-free living in the now
- worry not welcome in my healthy body
- fulfilled happy and peaceful
- belief in myself and my future
- enjoying every precious moment

I read that 90% of what we worry about never happens and the 10% that does happen is not the least bit affected by our worry. So why Worry? Also worry is like a rocking chair. It gives you something to do – but gets you **no** where!

# *Chapter Seven*

# Sample Spark Word Combos

## *From the 'Affirmation Doctor'*

**N**ow that you have a sample list of Spark Words including the ones you have created, let's design some Sample Spark Word Combos for you.

Learn how to string the Spark Words together to make powerful Spark Word Combos.

Look at the Picture index Card or recording device as you do the Spark Word Request Process.

Take your time with the process and become familiar with it. Experiment with exciting, new Spark Words and /or Spark Word Combos. This is your 'unique, individual, and Special Life Tool.'

At the beginning, when you start working with the Spark

Word Process, it is a good idea to keep it to yourself as sometimes remarks from others could discourage you. When miracles start taking place in your life, then please, by all means, share them with everyone!

## HOME STUDY

Some of my readers have started weekly Spark Word Combo Sessions in their homes and are thoroughly enjoying the interaction and fellowship. They cannot wait to hear the new and exciting miracles that other members are experiencing and sharing.

## SPARK WORD COMBO HINTS
## TO RECAP

Please remember to always take a few minutes and really think about what you wish to 'Spark' for. Be as specific as you can.

When your request is clear in your mind and you have decided your Intention for that particular Spark Word Request, make up your own Spark Word Combo Request.

Focus on the appropriate index Card repeating ALL the words on the Card 21 times in the morning and evening.

Do this process for *each* Spark Word Combo Request. Repeat each Spark Word Request before going on to the next one. When repeating your Spark Word Combo

Request, please be sure to add the 2 constant framewords at the top of the card, **Together** and **Miracle** to complete your Spark Word Combo.

Now let's start our Spark Word Combo Designs!

## NOTE

Be certain to glance over your Intention (Master Affirmation) **before** repeating your Spark Word Request 21 times every morning and evening for optimum success!

## HAPPY SPARKING!

*Spark Words When Properly Done, Always Work!*
*(Sometimes instantly)*

# BUSINESS

## SAMPLE INTENTION (Master Affirmation)
## PROSPEROUS HOME-BASED BUSINESS

I, (your name), deserve and now attract and enjoy a successful business. My business benefits all who come into contact with it. I have the funds and necessary education to operate and manage my own business.

I believe in my abilities and myself. My business increases monthly. I have in excess of ___ paying clients and/or customers daily that nets me in excess $_____ monthly. I am happy, prosperous and fulfilled to the good of all parties concerned. Thank you, thank you, thank you.

I fully accept.

Signed_____ Dated _____

Sample Spark Word Combo

TOGETHER MIRACLE
**PROSPEROUS HOME-BASED BUSINESS**

# CAREER

## SAMPLE INTENTION (Master Affirmation)
## CAREER FULFILLMENT

I, (your name), deserve and now have the perfect, lasting, successful, career, that gives me in excess of $_____ per month or year (net or gross). I use my creative abilities and gifts. I move from one great success to another.

I work in a harmonious environment and I am recognized and appreciated for my excellent work. I am happy and fulfilled to the good of all parties concerned. Thank you, thank you, thank you.

I fully accept.

Signed_____ Dated _____

### Sample Spark Word Combo

## TOGETHER MIRACLE
## CAREER FULFILLMENT

# CAREER
## SAMPLE INTENTION (Master Affirmation)
## PROMOTION AND RAISE

I, (your name), deserve and now have and enjoy my wonderful promotion with a substantial increase in pay. I use my creative abilities and gifts. I work in a harmonious, thriving and stimulating atmosphere.

I am appreciated and rewarded for my excellent work. I am healthy, happy and fulfilled to the good of all parties concerned. Thank you, thank you, thank you.

I fully accept.

Signed_____  Dated _____

## Sample Spark Word Combo

## TOGETHER MIRACLE
## PROMOTION AND RAISE

# HEALTH
## SAMPLE INTENTION (Master Affirmation)
## HEALING GRIEF

I, (your name), deserve and now am releasing my excess grief, sadness and sorrow. I go on with my life after my loss. I have courage and strength to move on and experience new things, conditions and people. I am becoming more and more peaceful. I ask for professional help when I feel that I need it.

I know grief is a journey and I make it through with the help of my Creator, loved ones and friends to the good of all parties concerned. Thank you, thank you, thank you.

I fully accept

Signed_____ Dated _____

## Sample Spark Word Combo

## TOGETHER MIRACLE
## HEALING GRIEF

# HAPPINESS

## SAMPLE INTENTION (Master Affirmation)
## HAPPY PLAYFULNESS

I, (your name), deserve and now have and enjoy peace of mind, joy, love and happiness every day. I live in an attitude of gratitude for my blessings. I am balanced, happy and peaceful.

I take time to enjoy the playful and fun times. I love spreading joy and happiness wherever I go. I share my happiness with others to the good of all parties concerned. Thank you, thank you, thank you.

I fully accept

Signed_____    Dated _____

### Sample Spark Word Combo

## TOGETHER MIRACLE
## HAPPY PLAYFULNESS

# HEALTH

## SAMPLE INTENTION (Master Affirmation)
## HEALTHY FOOD AND EXERCISE

TOGETHER MIRACLE

HEALTHY FOOD
AND EXERCISE

I, (your name), deserve and now attract and enjoy radiant health. I am becoming healthier and healthier every day. Every part of my body is working together to create health in my body, mind and spirit. I love walking in nature.

I am Divinely motivated to eat the right food and do the exercises that are tailored just for me to the good of all parties concerned. Thank you, thank you, thank you.

I fully accept

Signed_____ Dated _____

## Sample Spark Word Combo

### TOGETHER MIRACLE
## HEALTHY FOOD AND EXERCISE

# HEALTH
## SAMPLE INTENTION (Master Affirmation)
## PAIN GONE—HEALTHY STRETCHING

I, (your name), deserve and now am becoming healthier and healthier and pain-free. My body is working together in creating my healthy, balanced, pain-free, active body. I live in the now and I treasure each and every day. Nature is very healing to me. I am thankful for my many blessings.

I take time to meditate and I live in an attitude of gratitude for my blessings to the good of all parties concerned. Thank you, thank you, thank you.

I fully accept

Signed_____     Dated _____

### Sample Spark Word Combo

## TOGETHER MIRACLE
## PAIN GONE—HEALTHY STRETCHING

# HEALTH
## SAMPLE INTENTION (Master Affirmation)
## HEALTHY BLOOD PRESSURE AND EYES

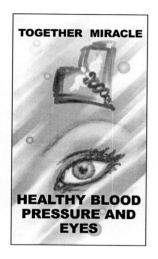

**TOGETHER MIRACLE**

**HEALTHY BLOOD PRESSURE AND EYES**

I, (your name), deserve, attract and now have and enjoy normal, healthy blood pressure and a strong, healthy heart. Every part of my body is becoming healthier and healthier. I enjoy perfect eyesight (20/20 vision). I see clearly now.

Any and all unwanted, negative stress leave my body, never to return to the good of all parties concerned. Thank you, thank you, thank you.

I fully accept

Signed_____ Dated _____

*Sample Spark Word Combo* for *reducing* your blood pressure – **TOGETHER MIRACLE – CUT B.P.**

*Sample Spark Word Combo* for *increasing* your blood pressure – **TOGETHER MIRACLE – RAISE B.P. TO NORMAL**

Sample Combined Spark Word Combo
TOGETHER MIRACLE
**HEALTHY BLOOD PRESSURE AND/OR EYES**

# HEALTH
## SAMPLE INTENTION (Master Affirmation)
## NEGATIVE FEAR RELEASED

I, (your name), deserve and now am completely free of negative fear. I am becoming healthier and healthier and I remain peaceful and at ease in fearful or stressful situations. I enjoy every day to the fullest. I walk in gratitude.

I close the door to negativity and open the door to health, love, joy and happiness. I am safe, secure and protected. Fear is not welcome in my healthy body.

I take time to meditate and relax to the good of all parties concerned. Thank you, thank you, thank you.

I fully accept

Signed_____ Dated _____

## Sample Spark Word Combo

## TOGETHER MIRACLE
## NEGATIVE FEAR RELEASED

# HEALTH

## SAMPLE INTENTION (Master Affirmation)
## COMPLETED MEDICAL TREATMENTS

I, (your name), deserve and now have all my medical treatments and procedures successfully completed. I am full of wonderful energy and faith knowing that I am becoming healthier and healthier.

I look forward to each new and wonderful day. I am healing completely and quickly from the inside out. Every part of my body is working together to create my pain-free, firm, healthy and balanced body to the good of all parties concerned. Thank you, thank you, thank you.

I fully accept

Signed_____ Dated _____

Sample Spark Word Combo

TOGETHER MIRACLE
**COMPLETED TREATMENTS**

# HEALTH

## SAMPLE INTENTION (Master Affirmation)
## HEALTHY IDEAL WEIGHT

I, (your name), deserve and now attract, have and maintain the perfect, ideal weight for me. I eat healthy food and engage in a special exercise program, tailored just for me, taking into consideration any medical challenges I may be dealing with. I am becoming healthier and healthier.

All **excess** fat and weight now drop from my body from the right places. My medical professionals are very pleased with my reduced weight and steady progress. I am happy, peaceful and fulfilled to the good of all parties concerned. Thank you, thank you, thank you.

I fully accept

Signed_____ Dated _____

Sample Spark Word Combo

TOGETHER MIRACLE
**HEALTHY IDEAL WEIGHT**

# HEALTH
## SAMPLE INTENTION (Master Affirmation)
## IMPROVED SELF-ESTEEM

I, (your name), deserve and now have and enjoy good, healthy self-esteem and self-approval. I believe in myself and my future. I release all thoughts of past failure. I now easily move on from one great success to another. I am lovable, loving and loved.

I am learning to love, respect, approve and accept myself just the way I am. I am becoming healthier, happier and more self-assured to the good of all parties concerned. Thank you, thank you, thank you.

I fully accept

Signed_____ Dated _____

### Sample Spark Word Combo

### TOGETHER MIRACLE
### IMPROVED SELF-ESTEEM

# LOVE

## SAMPLE INTENTION (Master Affirmation)
## UNCONDITIONAL LOVE

I, (your name), deserve and now attract and enjoy healthy self-respect, self-approval and Divine Love of self and others. I am a powerful Love Magnet to the right people and the right circumstances. I love spreading peace, joy and happiness wherever I go.

I am lovable, loving and loved. I am happy and secure to the good of all parties concerned. Thank you, thank you, thank you.

I fully accept

Signed_____ Dated _____

### Sample Spark Word Combo

## TOGETHER MIRACLE
## UNCONDITIONAL LOVE

# LOVE
## SAMPLE INTENTION (Master Affirmation)
### FAMILY LOVE

I, (your name), deserve and now create and have family harmony. I spread love, peace and joy to all family members to dispel any anger, misunderstandings and/or differences.

I love, respect and approve of self, family members and others. I am excited about greeting the brand, new day! I am a powerful Family Love Magnet to the good of all parties concerned. Thank you, thank you, thank you.

I fully accept

Signed_____    Dated _____


## Sample Spark Word Combo

### TOGETHER MIRACLE
### FAMILY LOVE

# LOVE

## SAMPLE INTENTION (Master Affirmation)
## ROMANTIC LOVE – RELATIONSHIP/MARRIAGE

TOGETHER MIRACLE

ROMANTIC LOVE

I, (your name), deserve and now attract, have and maintain the perfect, loving, healthy, happy, and lasting relationship/ marriage for me with my special romantic love partner. We love and adore each other. We enjoy safe, healthy sex. We live together in peace, joy and love. Each day is a new and wondrous experience.

The power of my subconscious mind knows where this person is and brings us together in its own special way. We are healthy, happy, secure and fulfilled to the good of all parties concerned. Thank you, thank you, thank you.

I fully accept

Signed_____ Dated _____

## Sample Spark Word Combo

### TOGETHER MIRACLE
### **ROMANTIC LOVE**

# MONEY/PROSPERITY
## SAMPLE INTENTION (Master Affirmation)
## MATERIAL THINGS

I, (your name), deserve and now attract, have and maintain abundant money /prosperity. I have extra money for children's education, traveling, cruising or just sitting back and enjoying life to the fullest. I am a powerful Money Magnet and I magnetize money to me.

I make good and wise decisions. I have the material things that I desire.

I am happy and fulfilled to the good of all parties concerned. Thank you, thank you, thank you.

I fully accept

Signed_____ Dated _____

Sample Spark Word Combo

TOGETHER MIRACLE
**MATERIAL THINGS**

# RETIREMENT

## SAMPLE INTENTION (Master Affirmation)
### HAPPY RETIREMENT

I, (your name), deserve and now have and enjoy great health, financial prosperity and happiness in my retirement. I make my retirement exciting and wonderful.

I enjoy every single moment. I live life to the fullest. I now do all the things I only once dreamed of doing.

I involve myself in interesting hobbies that I love and I find ways to help others. I am happy and fulfilled to the good of all parties concerned. Thank you, thank you, thank you.

I fully accept

Signed_____ Dated _____

## Sample Spark Word Combo

### TOGETHER MIRACLE
### HAPPY RETIREMENT

# SPIRITUAL GROWTH
## SAMPLE INTENTION (Master Affirmation)
### PERFECT PEACE

TOGETHER MIRACLE

PERFECT PEACE

I, (your name), deserve and now attract, have and maintain the perfect, ideal Divinely Guided life. I bask in the wonderful peace that surpasses all understanding. I move to higher Spiritual levels of understanding, peace and joy.

I fill my mind with positive, uplifting thoughts daily. I am peaceful, balanced and centered to the good of all parties concerned. Thank you, thank you, thank you.

I fully accept

Signed_____ Dated _____

Sample Spark Word Combo

TOGETHER MIRACLE
**PERFECT PEACE**

# *Chapter Eight*

# Weaving It All Together

Thank you for your interest in my unique, one-of-a-kind Spark Word Combo Process.

When using this powerful process for creating your desires, please remember to keep in mind the safety clause, 'to the good of all parties concerned,' and this includes You!

One reader asked me if she could use a Spark Word Combo to make her ex break up with his lady friend and of course my answer was, "No, we never say, write or do anything to hurt or take from another person."

Mary, a long-time reader of affirmations was having difficulty with a disgruntled family member and it was really making her upset and taking too much of her time so she decided to use the Spark Word Combo as follows: **TOGETHER MIRACLE--FAMILY LOVE**

She repeated this Spark Word Combo over and over even more than the suggested 21 times in the morning and evening. She was totally amazed and pleased that it worked so well.

Greg used Spark Words to receive a promotion and pay raise. He was the only one who was promoted and given a substantial raise. He is very excited and he is now using The Spark Word Process in all areas of his life with great success. He says some of the Spark Word Combos work quicker than others.

When you do this wonderful, *Magical Spark Word Process*, you will experience the excitement and amazement at how it quickly it works!

I firmly believe that this Spark Word Combo Process clears the pathway of all obstruction and/or any negativity so your desires manifest right before your eyes!

I have been searching for this simple, easy and effective process all my life and now I believe that I have found it!

I like to call this **MY MAGIC LAMP!**

**TOGETHER – LET'S LIGHT UP THE WORLD!**

Email:

annemarieevers@shaw.ca

Please share your Spark Word success stories with us!

**Happy Sparking!**

# **Much Love and Spark Word Blessings**

Dr. Anne Marie Evers a.k.a Dr. Spark!

*Spark Words When Properly Done, Always Work!*
*(sometimes instantly)*

# TESTIMONIALS

**Carole Matthews on Spark Words!**

Dr. Anne Marie Evers has done it again... this inspirational lady has been sharing her positive words with thousands of people via her books, lectures and weekly radio shows and also during her appearances on my weekly shows. 'Spark Words 'are her newest venue to guide people, and that they do! I am using them daily and am manifesting what I feel I deserve in my life. Give them a try ... they really work! Thank you, Anne Marie for all that you do!

*Love, Carole from Ontario, Canada*

I was having difficulty with some of my staff in my Hair Salon. First I wrote my Intention of exactly what I desired to take place. My Spark Word Combo was for staff harmony. Then every morning and evening, I would take out my Intention and glance over it and then say my Spark Word Combo 21 times for that particular desire. And it worked! I was so thrilled to see the way my staff began working together, being helpful to one another and I could just FEEL the difference in the whole atmosphere. I am very impressed with this successful, extra ordinary process.

*Thank you's from Karen, Owner of Hair Salon*

When my I-Pad stopped working I thought I would have to buy a new one. I learned about Spark Words and Spark Word Combos and I decided to try that process. I jotted down my Intention, glanced over it and all the way to the Apple Store I kept repeating over and over – **TOGETHER MIRACLE – COMPUTER FIXED**. It worked! One of the technicians fixed it for me quickly and no charge!

*Thank you, Dr. Evers, Deborah U.S.*

Since doing the Spark Word Process my finances have greatly improved. I am now working with two issues, my finances and releasing anxiety and both are working very well. Also I have more peace in my life.

*Cheers, Daniel, Toronto, Ontario*

I say the Spark Word Combos **TOGETHER MIRACLE – COUNTING IN** for the money coming to me and I happy to report it is working wonderfully!

*Annie Lynn, World Traveler*

All I can say is that you have hit onto a very successful formula here. My husband passed away ten years ago and I have not had a date for years. Just after I used these Spark Words, I had my first date. I am so excited and a little scared. I read when I do my Intention that I should use the safety clause – 'to the good of all parties concerned.' I feel more safe and relaxed as I know that includes me. Honestly, I don't know where it will go, but it is a great start. Can't thank you enough Anne Marie. One of your Interested readers,

*Sandra from Penticton, BC*

I used the Spark Word Combo to find a certain poem that my mother wrote years ago. I have been searching for it unsuccessfully for months. I used the Spark Word Combo to FIND the poem and I found it! You have a very successful teaching tool here!

*Regards, Gordon, Victoria BC*

Great News Dr. Evers! I did the Spark Word Combo, **TOGETHER MIRACLE – PULSE DOWN** to bring my pulse down and it worked and still is working! Thank you so much.

*Josie, one of your readers*

I wanted a part in a certain play and I wrote out and repeated my Spark Word Combo **TOGETHER MIRACLE – PART IN PLAY**, and I got not only 1 part, but 3 parts! **WOW!** Affirming Magic. And then I did another Spark Word Combo saying **MEMORY GOOD** and my memory has greatly improved! I feel as if I am 'on a roll' and I get shivers up my back when I think about it! I love you and your work.

*Anita, Bermuda*

I have been using your Spark Words for the ideal career for me. About a week after doing the process, I felt an urge to call a longtime friend. When we visited on the phone he shared with me that his company was looking for a person with my technical skills and the pay sounded great! Long Story – Short . . . I got the job! And I start next month!  I feel so relieved and happy. Thank you for coming up with such a great technique that works!

*Leonard from Seattle, WA*

Just a quick note—Does this Spark Word Combo Process that you teach actually work? You bet it does! I am living proof. I just got the best deal ever on the vehicle of my choice. Never thought it would happen but it did! I'm a believer!

*Cheers Joseph*

***Spark Words When Properly Done, Always Work!***
***(Sometimes instantly)***

# ABOUT THE AUTHOR

## *Dr. Anne Marie Evers*

Affirmations Doctor now also *known* as **Dr. Spark** – has been teaching and sharing her knowledge about the power of properly done Affirmations, Affirmation Life Tools, Positive Thinking; Goal Setting; Mind Power; Thoughts; Words; Forgiveness, Self-Esteem; Creative Visualization, and much more for the many years.

Ordained Minister
Doctor of Divinity
Member of the Canadian Guidance & Counselling Association, Vancouver, BC
Holds  an Honorary Degree in Psychology
Certificates in Child Psychology 212

### INTERNATIONAL MOTIVATIONAL SPEAKER

Canadian Conference Community Oncology (COCO'15) at Four Seasons Hotel, Whistler, BC sharing Affirmation Life Tools Help Cope with Negative Side Effects of Chemo and/or Other Medical Treatments from her book on June 20, 2015

### BOOKS

Best Selling Author of 14 books and numerous e-books on The Power of Affirmations -

Affirmations Your Passport to Happiness 8th edition

Co-Author with Dr. Deepak Chopra and Dr. Wayne Dyer
<u>Wake Up & Live the You Love Life in Spirit</u>
Just released – <u>AFFIRMATIONS LITE – The Bare Essentials</u>

## WORKSHOP FACILITATOR, LECTURER

Monthly Affirmation Lectures at Evergreen House

(Part of Lions Gate Hospital, North Vancouver, BC) sharing information from her most recent book,
<u>70 ways to Cope with Chemo and/or Other Medical Treatments</u>

Affirmation Lecturer *(10+years),*
Silver Harbour Senior Centre,
North Vancouver, BC

## RADIO/INTERNET

Weekly Radio/Internet Talk Show Host from Coast to Coast & Worldwide on the Web

## DR. EVERS BOOKS

www.annemarieevers.com, www.amazon.com

## WEBSITES

www.annemarieevers.com
www.annemariesangelchapel.com
www.heretohelpsolutions.com

# CREATE & EXPERIENCE THE MAGIC OF YOUR OWN SPARK WORDS AND/OR SPARK WORD COMBOS

The author gives the purchaser of this book permission to duplicate the following images to design your own Spark Word Cards

## NOTE

Print off the images. On the blank side of the image, jot down your INTENTION *(Master Affirmation)* – On the picture side type in **Together** and **Miracle** and then select what you desire **(YOUR SPARK WORDS)** as below.

Print on heavy paper or cardboard so you can carry it with you in your purse, wallet, gym bag, etc. You can read it when waiting for a friend, appointment, relaxing or whenever you have a few free minutes.

*Spark Words When Properly Done, Always Work!*
*(Sometimes instantly)*

# PRINT YOUR OWN
# SPARK WORDS

See – Anne Marie's Personal Spark Word Library
for Spark Word suggestions – page 45

**FRONT**

| |
|---|
| I, (your name), deserve and now have and enjoy peace of mind, joy, love and happiness every day. I live in an attitude of gratitude for my blessings. I am balanced, happy and peaceful. |

**BACK**

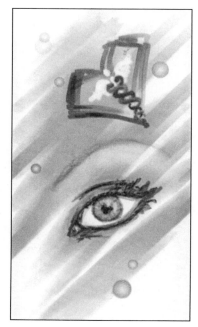

# SPARK WORDS TO GO

I LIKE TO
SPARKLE WITH
SPARK WORDS

I LIKE TO
SPARKLE WITH
SPARK WORDS

I LIKE TO
SPARKLE WITH
SPARK WORDS

I LIKE TO
SPARKLE WITH
SPARK WORDS

*Spark Words and Spark Word Combos
When Properly Done Always Work!*